Yellow Stars and Ice

PRINCETON SERIES OF CONTEMPORARY POETS
David Wagoner, *Editorial Adviser*

Yellow Stars and Ice

by Susan Stewart

Princeton University Press
Princeton, New Jersey

Published by Princeton University Press, Princeton, New Jersey
In the United Kingdom: Princeton University Press, Guildford, Surrey

Library of Congress Cataloging in Publication Data will be
found on the last printed page of this book

Publication of this book has been aided by a grant from the
Paul Mellon Fund of Princeton University Press

This book has been composed in Linotron Trump

Clothbound editions of Princeton University Press books
are printed on acid-free paper, and binding materials are
chosen for strength and durability

Printed in the United States of America by Princeton
University Press, Princeton, New Jersey

For Daniel Halevy

"N'apaisons pas le jour et sortons la face nue
face aux pays inconnus qui coupent aux oiseaux leur sifflet . . ."

Aimé Césaire, *Cadastre*

Contents

Grateful acknowledgment is made to the following magazines in which several of these poems first appeared:

The American Poetry Review—"The Drowned"

The Beloit Poetry Journal—"Four Questions Regarding the Dreams of Animals"

Kayak—"Every True Miracle," "The Doves Are Swallowing Wind," "The Summons," "Wish you were here," "Meaning to Drop You a Line"

The Paris Review—"The Carnival at the End of the Parade"

Ploughshares—"The Delta Parade"

Poetry Northwest—"The Long Boats of the Afternoon," "At Six," "The way the milkweed pods," "My City Knows How to Carry the Sky," "Terror," "Neighbors," "If I'm Homesick," "Yellow Stars and Ice"

Poetry Now—"My Ear to the Chest of the World," "In the Exact Middle of the Night," "The White Houses"

Prairie Schooner—"Letter Full of Blue Dresses"

My Ear to the Chest of the World

I put my ear to the chest of the world,
my ear to the pillow soaked
with dawn, and what returns
are the muted cymbals
of my own insomniac
heart, like someone
throwing glasses at a wall
all night and none of them
breaking. What a life my body
will carry on without me!
What enormous rivers
tearing free of the mountains.
It begins with the hoarse violin
scrapes of the sparrows
and the moon's slow dance
across the gleaming
white basin.

1 from the throw of hours

Every True Miracle

Every true miracle happens in the morning.
The heads and feet of our beds live on
and between them, our own heads and feet,
and between *them*, we say "It's us,
we're still here" with voices that haven't
cracked or split, that haven't changed keys
in the night. To brush our teeth is not
to destroy them. Only a little hair falls out,
hardly any skin comes off on the washcloth.
The inhabitants match the mailbox and the days
of the week are reliable. This is as astonishing
as orange juice, or soap that has risen
from ashes, as smooth and white as
an angel's hand and much simpler to believe in.
For the body never blows up. In spite
of heavy winds no limbs fall off. The birds
never wake up angrily, the milkman
walks on toes of tremendous kindness.
When it rains, the world doesn't melt,
and when it snows, the snow disappears
not the porch roof. Not a single building
has switched with another, not a single
bridge has buckled under by daybreak
with the weight of stars and buses.
The garden shakes off the dew like a puppy.
Light runs around the town without
a wheelchair, the church bells are acting
like acrobats. Even the mice survive!
A stranger is waking across the river
and by nightfall you may walk into his sleep.

The Long Boats of the Afternoon

Everywhere the long boats of the afternoon sail
in and out of the windows, dipping through
the low murmurs of mothers and children, pulled
by the sad August light on the shades. Imagine
blue hydrangeas shaking loose in a light rain,
a petal flickering like a startled moth, a white
moth disappearing into a white wall
and back, the wall folding into itself. And
out. It's only my cool hand and my white dress
in the water. It's only your single black shoe,
tap dancing around the room like a cricket.
Everywhere the afternoon comes swelling
through the windows, picking the locks
and prying open the bars like a grand
beginning that trails into a whisper or
an insect's song, rising in the heat. A yellowed
newspaper unfolds like a water lily and even
the news is news. Your black shoe is trying
its best to speak. The long boats drift slowly
by through the shadows, their blue flags
disappearing into the sky and back.
Their hulls are weighted by the trunks
of immigrants and prisoners, and by
lovers eloping with ropes and ladders.
A girl in the stern trails her hand through
the light, and the moon splashes out
like a flickering sheet of paper. And because
of this simple and absent-minded gesture,
she is the one who has written this poem.

At Six

for Edward Hirsch

Like a distant singing, like a finger sizzling
for just one moment on the iron, it almost
hurts. Almost. But then something pulls
away, and the smooth belly of evening
slides over the earth; the pines and the spaniels
stop howling and suddenly drop off to sleep.
While the air is numb with the drowsiness
of clouds, the needle sails free of the scars
on the record and the record player lifts
its artificial arm! This hurts.
But then a boy lays his cards on his bedspread
the way a sailor spreads his sails on
the sand, and even this reminds me
of tables being set, of a woman calling
and calling her children through blistered
hands. Then something lets go,
and in her left palm she sees her own eyes,
and in her right the evening's first star
pulls her toward the distant
singing of the sky. Then something else
lets go; the long sheet of night
winds slowly through the pines.
Here and there the lights
go up, like a shy applauding.

Ornament: The Towns of Sleep

The first and most important thing is
that they are never dark, that
wandering out of the evening through
the sashes etched in lead,
we come into a place fretted with
street signs and statues, the day
settling there on the alleys and the gardens
with the fresh and downy light
of a ripe bowl of peaches.
Against the wrought-iron stairs
and the gates to the small hotels,
desire's frail shoulders
are wrapped in her wide mantilla;
watch as the red geraniums slowly
part their lips, and the swaybacked
chestnut mare bravely dances
in place as she waits for the milkman.
The geese are glided over the lake by invisible
and mossy arms, but those still
wings on the moving surface
could be our arms, numbed
by the white waves of the sheets.

Here, my ear to your mouth,
I gather the distant music, and the street
lamps' shadows ride out on your breath
like a sigh. The violins burst
into flame with their passionate
hillbilly bows, while the sudden starts
and stops of the dead haunt us
like stammering children. Look at them
stepping there in the footprints
we never meant to leave behind.

Now the parade of the hoops and the sticks
and the jack-in-the-box begins,
the parade of the skeleton trumpets
rattling on the admiral's
chest. You cheer as the family
marches in like an old and exotic army,
dressed in their glittering costumes, their
hopes and their fleabag vacations.
The day's ragged pieces fall
like confetti from our vacant rooms,
and the corridors of dusk keep calling
us away from the center of the street.

Here, my mouth to your ear,
I can see the starry towns tucked
into the night's wide folds,
the hard eyes of a rabbit shining
awake in the hunter's deep pockets,
and the sea swelling and struggling
there inside the shell, gathering itself
into a furious whisper of
the towns within the towns.

In the Exact Middle of the Night

In the two rains falling on the middle of the night,
in the exact middle of the night between
the hood of a car slamming down its fist
and the cough of a motor,
starting from its bed, between the beggar
stumbling home with his pockets full
of light and the security guard carefully
pinning on his badge, his badge
like a frail cup of armor for his heart,
between the summons of regret and
the summons of courage, between the clock's
two good hands and its invalid voice,
between a blue breath going in and a gray
breath coming out, remember,
between two perfectly good and nourishing
rains, a phone rang twice and then
stopped. Like someone letting go
of a leash, letting a wild dog of love
run away in the heartsick rain,
or the way the tongue pulls back
from the dreamer's teeth,
then breaks in two like a dry
leaf with the burden
of its kisses.

The Black Tulips

The black rain filled the hands of every cup
and passed like a great wing over the earth.

The black rain fell with a fine and icy music, fell
through my fingers with its sooty light.

And in the morning the garden was as dark
and still as the moment before a match.

Everywhere the black tulips had raised their heads,
their martins' heads, slick and violet with remorse,

everywhere something had gone out; my black
hands were flickering between the needled trees.

Now I know that grief has no sense of its place,
that what's in my throat is as hard as

a bulb, pale with its cracking, its sudden
green voices. And I know that the earth

has no sense of our grief, that the wash
of rain is a kind of infection. Whenever I

wake I see the black tulips, their small fists
closing in defiance of the light, and whenever

I sleep it is the room unfolding into
the vast petals of the night. Those dark dresses

with their anxious hooks and eyes
are my dresses, glad to be free of

my body; that black wing folded against
my chest is my arm with her prisoner

dreams—all matches and keys. Because
the black rain fell with its terrible

handprint, because the garden cried out
with its icy music, because the night

holds our shadows like an armful of
flowers, glistening as if they'd been

picked in the rain, because our bodies have
a pale and a brittle cover, and our blood

is an ancient and clotted drum, I know
that my throat has lost sense of its voices

and that what infects us is all that remains.

2   the faces in the trees

The Delta Parade

Everything stops.
A fat man on his way to Baltimore
smokes for three hours in the club car.
The porter slips out and calls his wife,
he has one dime left and he's almost
yelling. Somewhere south of York,
she thinks he said. The funeral
procession leaves its lights on
and out of this pure stubbornness
its batteries go dead.
The bank robber leans on his horn
in desperation while his partner
snaps the rubber bands around
the money. A band,
you can hear it up the river,
first like the new heart of the child on
your lap, then like an old moon
pulsing below your nails, or something
softly moving through your arms and
throat. Here,
press here, not just drums.
A clown is throwing caramels
at the porch rails, balloons
are exploding or sailing up the river.
The lucky trees, to be able
to stand that close. If we talk
too much, we'll surely miss it.

And at the still center
of summer it starts; cowboys ride out
of another life, old cars get up
from the dead and dance
like cripples hired out for a tent meeting.
Up and down the sidewalk, the town
sucks in its breath like a girl
taking short gasps just above her trumpet,
or a fire engine's horn, heaving

like a drowned man or a heat wave slapping
against the water tower, this afternoon
just like a parade. The sore-footed
ponies are loaded down with flags
and the library float says
"Immortal Shakespeare," says it
with carnations and the hides of roses,
says it with a jester and a princess
wearing wings.

And she stutters, but no one cares
or can hear her. Except for the man
on the unicycle who tips his top hat
to the crowd, who swears he will
follow her anywhere, who follows
the mayor and the city council, who
follows the tap dancing class and the Future
Farmers, the Lions Club and the Veterans
of Foreign Wars; who clasps a carnation
between his teeth and sways
back and forth like
a broken clock.

And then things begin again,
a car follows the man on the unicycle
and suddenly it's just another car,
a pair of dice dangling
from the rearview mirror, a woman
giving her breast to a child and another
child carefully peeling a crayon, then
slowly giving the peels to his
grandmother, who opens the big brass
clasps of her pocketbook and lets
the bright curls drop slowly
to the bottom
like confetti or a boy's first
haircut. Like a first yellow leaf
that fell when we weren't looking.

Because it's summer. Like a smooth
yellow pebble that is rubbing and rubbing
in the new left boot of the drummer,
that someone skimmed on the river
exactly at three o'clock.
Not out of anger or of boredom
this time, but as if it could almost
wear wings.

Letter Full of Blue Dresses

Now the long evenings begin.
Two Amish girls are running
on the far side of the meadow.
A milk bucket joins their arms,
splashes frost on the thistle weeds.
Their dresses wrap around
their legs like ancient bruises, once
blue, now purple and black. Each
braid slaps the wind's face,
each thin leg stabs the frost.
This porch is the edge of
the world; I am not lying
when I say that to step
off the end of a plank like this
is to walk into another life,
where the first snow could enter
my skin, where the blue rag
thawing beneath the plum tree
would be the body I stepped out
of this evening. The stars
fly from the hayloft like
buttons from a serge dress,
like the dress I wore the day
the calf was stillborn,
the night the lightning tore open
the shed. I wake up constantly
to the sound of soft lowing,
to a clatter of shells
on the kitchen linoleum.
Two crows were killed
last week, chasing stars through
my window. I carried their
bodies from the slate roof
to the plum tree, burying
them under the frost. Their
thin legs seemed to point in
every direction. I have never felt
so lost as I did that morning.

For an hour I watched the water
pour into the sink
as if it were sky pouring out of
the faucet, or the blue cloth
a magician can pull from the fire,
as cold and silky as night.
Let me count the blue dresses
before sleep, anything to keep
from dreaming of the snow,
falling on my bed as if
it were a meadow where
two Amish girls carry a silver
bucket of milk and the thistle
weeds tear at their hems.
Blue dresses, step into me
as if I were frost, as if
the clothes that live beyond us
were more like veins than rags.
And the headlights that fly
across the walls this evening
were somehow necessary,
somehow needed, by the two girls
running on the far side of the meadow,
their dark feathers, their ancient light.

The Windmills

Someone taps a cigarette on the sill
and the sparks fly down like feeble
heartbeats. Tonight the doors yawn open
like the mouths of waitresses, each
waving in her sorry clients and bored
by the pinches, the changes of mind.
The windmills rise on the far horizon,
there like the arms of shivering children
holding their thin and silver pinwheels
against the frozen air. The closer
we come, the more they retreat,
their spokes winding forward,
then back and back while the grid
of sky is checked off behind them.
Water pours from the trough to the bucket
and the feedbags glide over and over
each other like the miller and his wife
rolling over in their sleep,
catching themselves between
the hopper and the wheel.
I can hear the furious wings,
paddling the sky above the thirsty prairie,
churning the clouds into knots and strings
and dizzying the rain-slicked crows.
It's the windmills that dance
to the night's jagged music
at the hour when the keys begin to bristle
in their locks, the hour when the sky's breath
hovers like a lecher around the reluctant
gas lamps; those are the windmills
that come back to me now, whirring
like the desperate inventions of a girl,
a waitress, who has suddenly leaped
from her bed. Pulled free at last from
the nightmare's arms, from the endless
and wooden turning.

In the Fields

I know the earth wants me and what it wants
is so easy to give, the way the silver maples
whisper behind their masks and the beetles
stitch the wounds of the furrows shut, the way
the crucifixion of scarecrows begins.
Yet every time I go outside, into the broken
air of March, or the air of September,
contaminated by night, I only
am convinced I am inside myself,
pulling up a little chair to a table
in the simple luxurious light
of my body.
                    The sun is the most exotic
and sullen thing I know,
there are days when the power lines
seem to faint across the hills, but
it's only my own mind
that has broken off
in the middle of a thin and feverish
sentence.
                    Sometimes I stop
and look down at my coat,
and I see another man standing
there, losing his breath and falling
over his shoes that are always too
large or too small; sometimes I see
my wife's breasts and thighs
and I know that the voice I wear
is hers.
                    Everything hides from
the light and yet I'd rather
be here than somewhere else;
the patriots of the town unfurling
their banners, the melancholy
rattling, the schoolteacher's rings.
There in the mica chips glinting from
the limestone are the daggers of a thousand
small deaths like these.

Why do they all expect
a confession, waving their arms at
the edges of the field?
Once in the first hour of morning
the clover swelled in an enormous
wave and in the froth that spilled
at its trembling mouth I saw
two seals leaping just beyond each other,
just beyond each other,
          then disappear.

The way the milkweed pods

No, the way a chicken watches his wings
lug his heart toward the woodpile and the great
red tear swells on his throat, nothing
ever dies simply. Your right hand torn with splinters
and your left hand freckled with blood, the way
you walk so slowly toward the woodpile and fold
the wings into the basin, no, nothing so simply,
each foot dragging a world behind the other.
Remember this, the way the milkweed pods
fly open with a shout, the way their white
wings sail out into the meadow with the sureness
of some immortal animal, sail out
on the stillest, most windless day of summer
when the crickets burn up with static
and a single hair sticks wetly to your cheek.
There is a little money beneath the carpet,
a little milk still cold in the bucket;
there are two blue letters in the mailbox
that think they are patches of sky.
This very minute the bread is rising on the table
with the unworried brow of a wise man.
The cows are out on the road again and in the parlor
Louise begins to play her violin, the name
of the song is "The way their white wings"
and the curtains are throwing lace roses
on her shoulders and her shoulders are aching
from holding up the song. There is a room
in the house you haven't found yet, where the ceiling
leans down to rest on the window and brushes
the hair from the eyes of a woman who sits there
all day sewing clouds to her apron.
She will lend you her needle to take out the splinters,
but when she tells you it's simple,
remember what I've said.

The Drowned

Listen to the song of the drowned,
who follow the water and never part
with it, those who hold their breath
in the small towns beneath
the reservoirs of Pennsylvania,
where on long September evenings
the carp lounge on the porch swings
and the dead float from house to house,
worrying rusted keys.
This is a song for those who drown
like assassins in bathtubs
of blood, and those who go down
in their sleep, laughing.
The drunken sailors who fall
from the piers, children who leap
into the shadows of mirrors, and
the woman who holds up the wreck
of her wrists, crying
"Look, cardinals!"
for the poet who makes his bridge
with white-knuckled fists.

A song of the Lorelei's smile
that made the morgues of Paris sigh,
the gambler's diamond pin
in the Mississippi mud,
the blackbird's abandoned spoon
and the broken glass of summer;
these artifacts of earth
shine from the blue floors of slate
quarries, spin from the fins
of the horizon's shark and weight
the clothes of the drowned.
This song is made where vapors
hiss above a pond, where kittens
hum in burlap sacks and
engines cough in the lake.

This is a song for the songs
of the drowned, who sing
of the lives that have passed
before them, who sing with
their eyes and their throats full
of sand, who burn with the fires
of swamps and deserts between
a chorus of water and land.

The Miners of Delta

In the anonymous night I see them,
in the shadows thrown on the house
by the random shouts of dogs and sirens,
in the breath of cars that rise and fall
on the wind and the radio beam's
slow cut through the roofs.
In the silhouette of the boy next door,
monstrous in the cap pistol's light,
and in my own eyes caught
between the window and the screen,
unable to turn toward the night, I
see them carrying their picks and
torches through the empty streets
of Delta; they are pulling
the stubborn quarry behind them
into the shattered light, into morning.

Everywhere they haunt the day,
in the checkout line at the supermarket,
and the lines at the movies and stations,
in the far seats of the subway
and the booths at the back
of the diner; everywhere the Delta
miners, silently watching
the living, drifting between
the slate's dull faces
that have somehow been broken into sky;
through the blue of the Susquehanna
and the marbled veins of their arms,
through the blue of their shirts
and their shoes and the heaving
blue of their lungs, they walk
with their twine linked around
their waists, their voices held
together by the heavy hymns of Wales.

In the drum of childhood bedrooms
and the startled voice of my husband
in his sleep, in the wall's electric hum
and the radiator rattling against the
dark, I hear their hammers and hatchets,
ringing the hours on the sides of the quarry,
blinding the water's eye below them
with the dust and smoke of their hands.
Here in the blanket's folds
are the bodies made of peat
and sandbags, here in the brooms
and the mops are the axes and chisels
of sadness; here are the Delta miners,
their faces chalked on the blackboard
night, chipping away through their own
throats and chests where their hearts
stand naked as diamonds or stars.

3 in the storefronts

My City Knows
How to Carry the Sky

Not the way the sky itself
holds a cloud, the sky
with its child's hands,
the cloud like a small
fish, slipping in and out,
not like the athlete
lifting a rock, showing
off his rocky muscles,
not like the dancer
who keeps his partner
from flying. No one
calls my city "champ,"
no one takes notice.
Not the workmen
with their pulleys
swinging a piano
and their hands
cupped over their eyes,
not the arab
with his arms full
of cantaloupes
and peaches, or
the shoeshine boy
with his shop on
his back.

There are the tired ones
who must carry everything
with them, the ones
who let everything fall.
There are mothers whose
arms grow long and sad,
carpenters whose tools
turn crooked and rusty.
There are the old ones
whose hearts split

open like almonds
with the weight
of each hard winter.
There are the houses
that finally drop
their windows, and
the girls who put down
their books and run,
while my city holds up
the sky, not with arms
or a head or a heart,
not even with patience
or a little courage, but
as if the sky were as
simple as breathing
and a city
could walk on its feet
like an ordinary man.

Terror

A man has died in the house next door,
rain pours through the open window
and the curtains flap their wet arms
on the bricks. Upstairs a phone rings
four times, for you. There is nothing
so prosaic as terror. Even as I write this,
a lamp is turned over, the debutante's
hair catches fire. The heroine breaks
her teeth on the tracks and hopes
that the train will loosen the ropes.
Wars break out in the subways,
and if I pick up the phone, I know
no one will answer, nothing so
voiceless as terror. A child
feels his mother's hammering
heart and swears he will never leave
the womb alive. Snow drifts slowly
on the insides of the windows
like the ponderous moaning of widows.
The piano refuses to rhyme.
Life as we know it runs out of our reach,
even as I write this, police fill the streets,
their horses limp along like battered children.
There is nothing so deliberate as terror,
like a wound that doesn't hurt and won't
stop bleeding, like a coat lined with guns
and razors, terror wounds us with its
silence and blindness, wounds us with
the calculated violence of lovers. Strangers
are tearing at your books and letters,
some are slitting your mattress with knives.
Even as I write this, blood soaks the feathers,
and the dead man stands behind you, terrified
by this poem. His skin is luminous
with rain and weeping, and he carries
his voice in his arms like a child.

Neighbors

The ones who live on the first story are torn
by little hungers. Their door stands open
to the avenue's voices, to the voices
that bark and march. There are chestnuts
and pretzels and a pig's head on a stick; a thin
rain of blood turns the corner to their
doorstep, where it scribbles the names
of those within. Remorse haunts their garbage
like a raccoon, whose sullen eyes
make them draw their curtains. Even in
daylight he stalks their alley. No one
can give them sleep; they hear letters falling
through the mail slot all night and brakes
squealing out like slaughtered animals.
Someone is always at the door,
no one is ever there.

The ones who live on the second story live
without memory or hope. There is a nest
of newborn sparrows outside the window;
their small heads are slick and raw and
they cry with no knowledge of the world.
Beneath the floor, voices scurry
like worried mice, and from the ceiling
fall the footsteps of the living and the dead.
In the morning and the evening they walk
between the walls, like gossip that goes
so far, before it steps out of
its voices. To the ones who live
on the second story, the windows are
stained and infinite mirrors where they
see themselves nested inside their rooms,
nested without wings, without wind.

As bottles are corked and thrown into the sea,
as glad chimneys puff a final anger into
the welcoming air, the ones who

live on the third story send their clothes
up into the sky. Up from the television
antennas and the whirring fans, up
from abandoned bricks and cement, and
the glass that burns with the sun on its
edges, they climb, their sheets knotted
around their waists, their clotheslines
scarring the clouds. The suicides and
the maniacs, the painters and the bats,
perch on the third story windows and slowly
let go of the earth. A jet comes ripping
across the ceiling and the sky writing says
"jump, yes, jump"

Things Get Harder

The wood turns up
its pockmarked face
and the hammer bounces back,
shocked and alone.
I tell you, each time we
reach out for our change,
the cashier puts her empty
finger in our palms,
her sour finger, twisted
like a little club, and none
of us will let her in.

Tonight the low ringing
of the sirens bounces
through the dark like
a hoop, and across
the pond at the edge of town,
the stars pull their net
with its catch of the drowned.
Those heavy limbs left
glistening on the shore are
our limbs, still swimming
away from morning.

What is it that we hold in
our thoughts and our pockets,
what keeps calling us down
to the mud? Everywhere
the knives leave their shadows
on the tables, as deep
and sullen as scars.
Our poor breath begs
to turn cartwheels in the wind,
but the rack of trees breaks
our words into pieces.

No, the somber milling of
the crows at evening does not
resemble a cakewalk
and the promenade of the generals
steps a little higher each day.
What we throw away,
I'm afraid, is what
we eventually need,
and things get harder as luck
would have it, as luck
will again let us go.

How the River Climbed Into this Poem

It is raining across my forehead and down
    my nose and into my mouth
and it is raining across the roof and over
    the eyebrows of the house, catching now
and then in the gutter's upper lip. It is raining
    on my neighbors and on the stranger's
furtive looks, raining on the Baptist hymns
    of the broomseller and his little brother;
it is raining down the pole of the barbershop, too,
    and up the stripe on the back
of the highway. It is raining and raining on City Hall
    and the ambitions of lunch dates
and divorces; even raining on the river, on
    the swimming pools and showers, raining
like a faucet on the pond's icy cheeks.
    It is raining on forsythia raincoats
and on mattresses left sleeping in the garbage,
    raining a revenge on the hardware store
and scattering the zinnia and squash seeds. It is raining
    right now on the dogwood tree
behind the empty house on Berks Street, raining
    on the wallpaper rosebuds there
until everything bursts into bloom. It is raining
    on the Mennonite graveyard and on the
delicate cemeteries of Fishtown, raining on the names
    of the dead and the flamboyant pseudonyms
of the living. It is raining on the trashbag's
    shining skin and raining on the pigeon's
matted feathers, raining on the sweet potato pies
    and the golden earrings of the vendors.
It is raining pennies and cats and dogs from heaven
    and raining the history of the future; it is
raining the great floods of Johnstown and Noah
    while the ballet of accidents begins.

It is raining in great sobs and single tears and raining
in the night shift's restless sleep, raining
through the haze of tomorrow afternoon and the languorous
picnics of July. And then, as if
a baton had been lifted and not at all like lightning or
thunder, it stops as soon as it's begun.

The White Houses

Here are the white houses at daybreak,
a long street of white houses
like a caravan of brides.
And over them, the moon
stands as calm as a choirmaster
or a piece of threadbare furniture,
left when the stars left town.
A little wind washes against
the blinds while the telephone
lines start to prowl through
the elm leaves. There in
the first childish steps of
the light, her arms flying
out to these threadbare
trees, the whippoorwill
patiently mocks my voice,
sucked dry by the sallow
cheeks of night.

The Doves Are Swallowing Wind

Night of the iron's sour clang,
night white with heat. In the factory
three men step back from the furnace
and suddenly notice each other's faces,
the foreman who wears the tattoo of the dead,
the engineer who sweats with salt and blood,
the apprentice who is drinking the light's
thick milk from a black and broken glass.

The streets are tired with the weight
of the homeless and the homeless are
tired of the streets. They yearn to sleep
in the peaceful ambulance, whose voice
is caught in the trees, who limps along
on two wheels and a whisper.

The pallbearers of the moon have arrived,
have filled the air with their drunken breath.
They are turning the windows inside out,
and I step back suddenly at the sight of my face,
at the sight of this poem, walking out
through the glass.

Melancholy night, I pull you, sleepwalking,
into the harbor like a great freighter
of dreams, like a tired fish who has borne
too many children, like a piece of iron
from the mouth of a furnace where two men
look away from each other, one who sweats
with salt and blood, one who wears
the tattoo of the dead. Your hull is full
of amnesiac sailors, your mast wears the veils
of brides and widows.

The doves are swallowing wind.

What is happening in the junkyard is happening
all over. The schoolbus stretches a broken arm
and rubs its headlights in surprise.
The sailors wake up in a crush of strangers,
in a bed of wet clothes and rotten wood
and can hardly remember they are sailors,
never mind the moon and the sea.

A wife sticks a tentative foot from the sheets
and watches her husband walk out through the glass.
He has stuffed her dream in a yellow pillowcase
which he carries, wiggling, on his back.

The ambulance goes around in circles,
like a patient amputee alone in a rowboat,
whispering "Taxi, taxi" to the deserted streets.
For the homeless have all gone home. The rapists
and waitresses have put on their uniforms. The moon
is pushed back into the furnace with all the strength
the foreman can manage. Its white heat catches
in his hair, and the walls are tattooed
with the shadows of the dead.

Exhausted night, broken at the waist,
bereft of your veils and anchors,
I drink from your black and shattered glass
with the heavy gestures of the sleepless,
with the tired heart of the engineer,
the heart of the apprentice and the wife,
who have all gone back to their beds.
To a sleep as dark as the empty harbor
where the doves are swallowing wind.

4   the streets confuse themselves
        with rivers once

Baltimore

Let me give you the time of day
when I'm walking around the languid hips
of the harbor, when the timothy weeds
and the phlox are bleached
in the sun and the rain; here, where
the torn faces of the melons accuse us
from every gutter and the tired donkeys
are balking at the bells and the gilt of
the fruit carts. A tramp snores on the sidewalk
by the theater with his left arm flung
around the shadow of his death, as tenderly
as the arm of any careless husband.
And above him, the marquee
blurts out *pure as the driven snow.*

Look how the women in their cotton dresses
come out like planets the colors of night
or like childless and exhausted immigrants
cast up from another life. They put their feverish
cheeks against the marble cold steps
while the alleys are rocking in the salty air
like solemn and empty cradles.
Once, riding up Charles Street, a man
leaped to his feet and shouted, "This bus
is headed for the Kingdom of the Lord,"
and the shoppers put their white gloves
to their mouths like astonished mimes.

Think of the hopeful gestures of that man,
laying out his trousers and socks, and his clean
white shirt, at midnight, of the dark
closing its hand around his bed as calmly
as a benediction, or how the widow arranges
the corpse's limbs with patient
deliberation; when she puts the lilies
to the back of the vase we can finally
see the asters. Lie down softly

on the cool stripes of the mattress like
a prisoner, naked and alone at last, and know
that each time someone pulls a chain on
a single bulb in a furnished room, another
invisible star invisibly explodes
over Baltimore.

Two Allusions to
the House of Walt Whitman

the parrot, who scratched the cherries from the clock

There was a time when I had wanted
everything to be perfect, the heavy-headed
lilacs drifting off at noon and the slow chimes
rising like the soft clap clop of horses.
My language was a curse on the rainbow
of my feathers, a hammer lopped across
a calloused ivory keyboard. My keyboard,
my ivory beak! No one understood
my confusion; I thought the biscuits
were part of a ritual of war and the bars
of my cage were a general's stripes.
I thought the hellos and so longs of
the citizens were a happy calling
of beasts. My hunger spoke Spanish
and wore a white suit, and I
blamed my fever on gold and nostalgia.
I could have sworn that the voices
outside the window were mocking
my folded wings. The night of the crime
I dumped the aspirins in the lilacs
and each branch unfolded like
a bird-of-paradise.

the clock, its cherries scratched off by the parrot

History with its back and forth
and forth and back until then
had never taken any skin
off my back. I loved to sing
with the horseless trolley, to
sing at the full swell of evening;
there when the clerks put their pens
back in their bottles and the morning
glories folded like Japanese papers.
The ladies straightening their velvet
bonnets came and went like little fish
in the clear pool of my glass.
They always surprised me with their
throaty laughs and their enormous
erotic cameras. Once I heard
the cook scrape the bottom of
the soup pot and I knew that I
had perfectly timed a heavenly
new world. But Camden was stricken
with a taste for the exotic and the parrot,
alone one starless night,
chewed the cherries off my breast.

The Countries Surrounding
the Garden of Eden

Pison, where *there is* gold

First they took the cedars and the larches,
dragging them away by their needles and
cutting them off at the root,
and who would have known that their satin
and green could line our path like thorns?
Then they took the flowering figs and the maples;
the petals that filled the air with sweet wings
stung our eyes and our hands.
At autumn's golden pitch
they came with their fire and their
sickles, and even the orchards
unclenched their fists, dropping their arms
into the crackling grass. And the things
that once grew as we grew,
now changed without changing,
like the sand and the wind.

Gihon, that compasseth the whole land

At the first frost we found
our sheep with strangled
hearts, lying on their backs
in the frozen clover, their eyes
wide open as if they were surprised
by a constellation of drought
or endless winter. The wolves
walked into the snow, like men who
have given up living without love;
cows would no longer let go
of their calves, hiding them deep
in the birch groves. Everywhere
the roads gave off their animal
cries, running toward the edge
of what we had thought was the world.
And the names of things as we knew them
would no longer bring them to us.

Hiddekel, that *is* it which goeth toward the east

It began with the wells, coughing
their last drops and the fish with
blistered scales that were
thrown up by the river.
We left each day with empty
nets and ropes, for
our bodies seemed to lose
their way home. Candles
and tallow disappeared from our
cupboads until every house
came to live in darkness. The night
lost its noises one by one and
the silence filled us with a fear
of glass and strangers. That spring
no salmon or swallows returned, and
the river moved restlessly under
its ice, like us, like magicians
who forgot what came next.

Euphrates

Then one day when the sea
was as still as the sky and
the horizon disappeared within
its own folds; when every
nest had been emptied and scattered
and brambles and cobwebs
tore at our faces; when
our plows and our wheels
lay broken in the dust and our
instruments were like mute
and obedient children; when
our children no longer spoke
our language and our own
tongues were like stones,
sharp against our lips,
we dreamed of a country
far up the river, where a man
and a woman stood naked
in a garden, their faces
naked of memory.

Take Today

for example, the mime troupe of the stars retreating
into the sky's pale wings, and the light
casting up the sleepers at last
on the littered beaches of their dreams.

The first trolley lumbers past the house, shaking
the cones from the larch tree, and just beyond
the garden walls, where the night still
crouches with its thieves,

a gray dove coos from the woods of New Jersey,
murmuring in the drowsy light
a "who" and a "you."

The way bonfires and firecrackers explode
a sadness as hot as fear or October
afternoons, something grows on us slowly, then
disappears, leaving the electric

charge of our blood leaping that much harder and
higher in our veins and throbbing through
our hearts and our hands; not like the lost song
that you want to remember

but the one that starts brightly and then unravels,
the pianist saying "wait a minute"
then wiping her brow, and beginning bravely once again.

Look how the little victories of the day
slowly take out their banners, how the white cloth
is spread and the cards are splayed, look
how the poppies that bank the highway

have stolen the hard conversations
of lovers. You can see them now, caught
in their silent hours while
the morning presses

its tired weight against the windshields.
Something could break
with the desperation of a bird on a string, or a gray
dove trapped in a picture of home,

but the garden stretches in the waking light
with the pitch and roar of a buried sea
and everywhere the wires sing in a single voice,
take today, take it up
while it wears your name.

How Long Does It Take?

Almost anything can happen between
the snap of the trigger and the bullet's
solitary exile across the ox-eye
daisies, the moment when our ears
bend down like polite and innocent
questions, saying, yes, I heard it,
or "the terrible hunger of the clouds."
The lightning slowly rips
through the silky night, while
the maples cross and uncross
their naked legs like embarrassed
girls. You feel the catastrophe
of the air raise the soft hairs on
your arms, the wind now struggling
at the back of your throat
like a captured bird. The dinner bells
are all set off at once by a careless
burglar, and the men put down their
hoes and rakes and start across
the fields. You know what they will say
when they reach their empty kitchens,
how the waiting rooms smell of
urine and death deep in the throats
of the hallways. And how hard
it is to forget a sudden vision
of the river, there without beginning
or destination and grazed with
the swollen twilight.

Four Questions Regarding the Dreams of Animals

1. Is it true that they dream?

It is true, for the spaces of night surround
them with shape and purpose, like a warm hollow below
the shoulders, or between the curve of thigh and belly.

The land itself can lie like this. Hence
our understanding of giants.

The wind and the grass cry out to the arms
of their sleep as the shore cries out, and buries
its face in the bruised sea.

We all have heard barns and fences splintering
against the dark with a weight that is more than wood.

The stars, too, bear witness. We can read
their tails and claws as we would read the signs of our
own dreams; a knot of sheets, scratches defining the edges
of the body, the position of the legs upon waking.

The cage and the forest are as helpless in
the night as a pair of open hands holding rain.

2. Do they dream of the past or of the future?

Think of the way a woman who wanders the roads
could step into an empty farmhouse one afternoon and find
a basket of eggs, some unopened letters, the pillowcases
embroidered with initials that once were hers.

Think of her happiness as she sleeps in the daylilies;
the air is always heaviest at the start of dusk.

Cows, for example, find each part of themselves
traveling at a different rate of speed. Their bells call back
to their burdened hearts the way a sparrow taunts an old
hawk.

As far as the badger and the owl are concerned,
the past is a silver trout circling in the ice. Each night
he swims through their waking and makes his way back
to the moon.

Clouds file through the dark like prisoners through
an endless yard. Deer are made visible by their hunger.

I could also mention the hopes of common spiders:
a green thread sailing from an infinite spool, a web, a thin nest,
a child dragging a white rope slowly through the sand.

3. Do they dream of this world or of another?

The prairie lies open like a vacant eye, blind
to everything but the wind. From the tall grass the sky
is an industrious map that bursts with rivers and cities.
A black hawk waltzes against his clumsy wings, the buzzards
grow bored with the dead.

A screendoor flapping idly on an August afternoon
or a woman fanning herself in church; this is how the tails
of snakes and cats keep time even in sleep.

There are sudden flashes of light to account for.
Alligators, tormented by knots and vines, take these as a sign
of grace. Eagles find solace in the far glow of towns, in the small
yellow bulb a child keeps by his bed. The lightning that scars
the horizon of the meadow is carried in the desperate gaze
of foxes.

Have other skies fallen into this sky? All the evidence
seems to say so.

Conspiracy of air, conspiracy of ice, the silver trout
is thirsty for morning, the prairie dog shivers with sweat. Skeletons
of gulls lie scattered on the dunes, their beaks still parted by
whispering. These are the languages that fall beyond our hearing.

Imagine the way rain falls around a house at night,
invisible to its sleepers. They do not dream of us.

4. How can we learn more?

This is all we will ever know.

5   a window flies open

The Summons

I call you friend from the tree houses and caves,
from the soft moss by the animal graveyard,
from dove's wing and dog's belly beneath,
and friend from the spruce at evening where
the swing and the wind are the same in the branches
and each whispers a name not its own, friend from
abandoned houses where an open suitcase
fills with rain and real birds peck the birds
from the wallpaper, friend even from this.
From the spaces between rooms I call you,
from songbooks full of wasps in the attic
and the pockets of your father's uniform, friend
from sharp bullets and feathers. I call you with
the barber's clicking teeth as your first hair
falls to the floor. I call you with the tongue
of the lizard in the springhouse and the bull's tongue,
raw on the salt lick. I call you with the bugler's
lips, with the lips of your oldest beloved,
I call you from the drum of the factory where
the carpenters hammer their thumbs. I call
you from the barn's darkest corner with
the language of spiders and cats. I call you
with the last key of the dismantled piano, with
the whistle of the child who can't whistle and
the tambourine of the man who is deaf and
dumb. I call you friend from the mirrors
and rivers, from the deepest most solitary
silences of sleep.

Wish you were here

Where the city falls
into the river's arms and the cars
are torn apart by the light,
here where the straw and the cats

disappear. How it happens
is a mystery to me.

The blue herons seem at home
by the fountain. Each day I
bring them a pocket's worth of almonds.
The river seems to rise a little

every morning, but so far
nothing has been broken.

Yesterday I saw a school
on the farthest island, but it was only
a chain being thrown against
a flagpole. By noon today the chain
had turned into a moth
and the flagpole was a small brass
lamp on my bureau.

Even that won't go out.

I had to paint all the windows
black, it's the only way
to get any rest. Here all the doors
have secret names

and the castles on the beach
are, I'm sure, true castles.

I met a woman
who makes her living waking
sleepwalkers. She said,
"In all the world they are the most
ungrateful. It's better to work for the dead."
A white speck in her left eye
seemed to grow larger. I know you think

I imagine these things, but the fear
I sometimes feel is still fear.

The shadows of the clouds,
spilled on the mountains, are as solemn
as the pacing of monks
in a garden. You must know

how unnerving this is. Lightning
comes and goes, estranged from its thunder.

I haven't prayed for anything in months,
not rain or affection or a fence
out of my childhood, or the tourists who fall
off the mountain every week

yet I have wished for you so often,
you are almost here and in the halflight

the shadows are bearing you in.
They are hatless and it's raining,
you are singing on their shoulders
and I have slipped this postcard

upside down in any book.

It's All You Said It Would Be
and More

Antelopes, for instance, seem to be everywhere
     and the sharp husks of acorns they spill on the walks
     had my boots broken in in no time at all.
Butterflies often rise up before me as startling and
     blue as handclaps.
Civility is no stranger to the natives here. Often
     I've walked in the early evening led only by
     the anxious light of their porches.
Don't misunderstand me, the darkness is a pocket
     that already has been shaken of its stars and its
     worries.
Everyone seems to know me by now, it has something
     to do with my accent. Being
foreign, though, is little more than an accident and
     doesn't seem to count much here.
Gentle as the wind is, it too speaks a tongue
     that sometimes hurts our ears. Do you remember
     how you used to think it
haunted our room and filled the pillows with more
     than water or
illusions? The suspicions of home are behind us now, but
jaded as that was, you were right.
Knowing the difference between night and day
     escapes me more and more each evening.
Let this always be the time between us, the hour
     when my pen staggers toward you.
More than before, I see there's always something
new, something else going on in the pendulous
orchards. There was a moment when I thought
     that they would blossom into winter and the snow
     would follow like modest little sisters. You see
pears can be as orderly as metronomes or
questions, striking in this
raw light of dusk.
Soon I will be caught in the rainy months
     that are always near our

thoughts of home. Alarms go on,
unnoticed, in the distant
villages where
we've hidden our boats and our paddles.
Examples are hard to come by; only
you know the way the tropics
zigzag toward our summers.

If I'm Homesick

It's a mockingbird in the elm tree
and a shred of yellow string sent sailing
by the woman on the second story
porch who is beating her soft white rugs
on the porch rails. So if I'm homesick
it's because there is no woman, no mocking
bird, not even an elm tree, but just a shred
of yellow string that falls into the snow,
like a scar that walks away from its wound
the sky can't stop up its silence.

It's a girl getting on the train to Boston
with a live goose stuffed head first
in her basket. And the baker swearing softly
in Portuguese as he puts a yellow egg inside
a yellow braid of dough and thinks about the girl's
yellow braids, about the train and the slapping
of rugs on the porch rails. A slap, and the flour
flies up like an angry goose! Or snow from a mocking
bird's wings, shivering in the brittle elm

Outside my window. But there is no mockingbird,
no elm tree, and like a blind man blinded by sight,
the sky can't bandage its sobbing. And if I'm homesick
it's the rattle of porches in my voice, a lung slowly
filling with snow. The children collapse
like a rosary in the schoolyard; their coats
take the shape of the wind and sail off.
The nuns have come out to scatter bread on the sidewalks,
blessing each piece with a prayer for the dead.

But don't mistake these for acts of mercy.
For the ghosts can't find their way if the birds
have eaten every crumb. And the mockingbird
will never find his voice if the birds lose their way
in the whiteness. And if I'm homesick it's a window

shrouded with ice where a young girl traces a name
on the glass that's beginning to look like my name.
It's the sky taking shape before me in the silence
like a ghost who makes nothing come true.

The Souvenirs

Where are the bruises and the elegant scars of everything
we've put behind us?

Where the snow waits patiently at the bottom
of the sea beside a miniature cathedral of Ys,

we see ourselves tasting the cold designs of a world
that once melted on our lips. Give me a graveyard

in a glass cup and I will prove it is always
snowing, that the train leaping through

my heart like a stallion is only the toy
of an invalid orphan, inventing the world

from the mountains of his bed. Look, the countries
that rise there in his sheets are our own

shadows thrown from his feverish walls.
The maids of the grand hotels anxiously wait

for our postcards. I can see them polishing
their glasses and silver and rubbing

the sleep from their eyes. Sparks fly
from the slender windows, from the friction

of their patience, while their shoes wear against
the carpets and their hands wear

against each other. The souvenirs stand
at attention in the shops, gleaming like the shapely

and golden maps of a city that has risen
in our dreams. The saintliness of pencils

and broad-brimmed hats fills us with longing
for a place we've never seen, for the hidden rooms

of another language; to wake at sea
or beside an open window is more than we've

ever hoped for. Something smoulders
inside us and refuses to go out, like a tiny pin

left aching in a hem or a hot splash of coffee
on a pale new dress. These things burn forever

through the velvet dark of the closet.
Remember how the perfect order of the days

can be spilled on a well-worn carpet, and though
the landscape has only changed a little, it can

leave out everything we loved.

Meaning to Drop You a Line

Monday the peddlers threw their scarves into the water
and I knew it was the beginning of something finished,
polished at the edges and blue as a razor, you can picture
all that silk as it started to rain.

And it's been raining ever since. On Tuesday we covered
the summer furniture and put the mannequins back
into their alcoves. With little thought to our own
comfort, we went ahead and stripped the awnings.

The sun has shot us full of lead and salt; I feel it
tunnel through my tongue each evening. Wednesday
night the pipers picked clean the beaches and
the town kids were out there with their flutes.

Why is there no new music? asked the guests. By Thursday
the sharks rolled in like playing cards; their confidence
always surprises me. The accordion player has hurt
his leg, but he still can tumble the high notes.

Around the clock Friday we watched the regatta and the war
was the farthest thing from our thoughts. Remembering
the careful way the waves break behind us, "like a
comb through a part," we said, handing out the ribbons.

And everyone got one. The weeks are full of Saturdays
and singing. The shutters started banging before we could
stop them; we haven't seen the end of the tailor and
his sister. It is said they are traveling under names

They have assumed. I knew as much Sunday when the dock
had drifted and weary valises covered all the carpets.
Through the blinds this morning I could see a red convertible,
its door hanging open like the silence before a knock.

Yellow Stars and Ice

I am as far as the deepest sky between clouds
and you are as far as the deepest root and wound,
and I am as far as a train at evening,
as far as a whistle you can't hear or remember.
You are as far as an unimagined animal
who, frightened by everything, never appears.
I am as far as cicadas and locusts
and you are as far as the cleanest arrow
that has sewn the wind to the light on
the birch trees. I am as far as the sleep of rivers
that stains the deepest sky between clouds,
you are as far as invention, and I am as far as memory.

You are as far as a red-marbled stream
where children cut their feet on the stones
and cry out. And I am as far as their happy
mothers, bleaching new linen on the grass
and singing, "You are as far as another life,
as far as another life are you."
And I am as far as an infinite alphabet
made from yellow stars and ice,
and you are as far as the nails of the dead man,
as far as a sailor can see at midnight
when he's drunk and the moon is an empty cup,
and I am as far as invention and you are as far as memory.

I am as far as the corners of a room where no one
has ever spoken, as far as the four lost corners
of the earth. And you are as far as the voices
of the dumb, as the broken limbs of saints
and soldiers, as the scarlet wing of the suicidal
blackbird, I am farther and farther away from you.
And you are as far as a horse without a rider
can run in six years, two months and five days.
I am as far as that rider, who rubs his eyes with
his blistered hands, who watches a ghost don his
jacket and boots and now stands naked in the road.

As far as the space between word and word,
as the heavy sleep of the perfectly loved
and the sirens of wars no one living can remember,
as far as this room, where no words have been spoken,
you are as far as invention, and I am as far as memory.

The Carnival at the End of the Parade

I want to tell you, it has nothing to do with
trees or luck, that the last carnations crumbling in the gutter,
the float stripped down by the rain, even the drum major
and the fireman, lifting their beers to the moon, are part of some
other show, some other season, which the barkers have never known.

Not that it isn't July, not that we didn't expect it,
our names are carved in the muscles of the ringmen, our faces
are loud on the sleeves of the clowns. A small town's talk is dry
on our tongues and only this sawdust can soothe it. This is meant
as fair warning; our tickets are as sharp as teeth.

I want to tell you how the heart flies out of the body,
how the wind fills a ragged arm, how the screams and cries
at the top of the coaster have nothing to do with the earth.
How the rainbows caught in the glasses are the hallucinations
of lanterns. How a yellow hound sings by the tent post

And his song is the song of lions. Listen, the music
here is not music, but the creaking of strippers with their
metal hips, the crackle of wires that rear and spark like horses,
the hiss of smoke from the mouth of an evening, wide and swollen
with kisses. I want to come right out

And tell you, that mouth is my mouth, and it throbs
with every word. How the strippers are frightened by thunder,
how they flinch at the sound of applause, how the gesture
of the clown as he's hit with the baseball moves the audience
to sob and throw flowers.

How those flowers land softly in the laps and hair
of the veterans playing Bingo in the shadows; how their rings
are flashing like knives, and the spinning cage holds too many
letters; how as soon as someone wins, someone disappears
with cards and buttons flying.

Listen, the things that happen here don't just happen.
The horses hold fast to the merry-go-round because there's
nowhere better to go, but if some night a small girl whispered
"Venus" in their manes they would take off toward the sky.
And the Ferris wheel, packing a suitcase,

Would tumble after them "head over heels," which
is not a name for love or confusion but simply the way things go
when every exit to town is jammed and the air is close with
animals, when the fire-eater drinks with the fireman and
the rafflers start counting the trees.

And this is my only chance to tell you—how
the body can fly from the heart, leaving it there like a soiled
red kerchief on the neck of a god in his shirtsleeves, the one
with the strength to pull the levers that lift a whole town
to the stars.

6   once a starling hits the glass

The Dedication of Sleep

Each night I fall asleep
in honor of the dead, in honor
of the green-shooted irises.

Here in the small and enormous
cup of night, my sleep spills
over like my hair on the pillow.
Or something more familiar,
the bloodstains of the moon.

The train of the dead crawls from Rome
to Arezzo with the slow-witted
innocence of a child. The train
of the dead is naked, naked
without kerchiefs or flags.

I fall asleep in honor of the rain,
in honor of the restlessness of leaves,
and a great stirring passes
over the earth; it is the music
of our forgetting.

The train of the dead leaves
on Wednesdays and hardly
ever returns.

Sleepwalkers, pay attention to this
sorrow, this honorable sorrow that
reads over my shoulder, that stands
in the shadow of every doorway
and seems to bear me no ill.

Where are the women who
throw up their skirts, their
red slips, their happy blindfolds?

In the train of the dead there
is no dancing, no wealth
and no beginning.

I fall asleep in honor of the living
rain and my sleep winds through
the mountains of night like
a terrible fugue of rivers.

It is the eyes that are swollen
at the end of sleep,
the bashful eyes against
the morning's striptease.

The train of the dead has a flute-
like whistle, a far whistle
and no silences.

If you open the windows in the train
of the dead, the air rushes in
then out with alarm.
If you turn back a corner of the earth,
it will cover its face with its hands.

The way a bride turns and fusses
with her long net veil,
this train takes up
her tracks behind her.

Each night I fall
asleep in honor of the flower
girls who scatter
the green-shooted irises.

And since I sleep with nothing
in my hands, since I sleep
inside this human egg,
this wealth of eggs inside me,

the bits of mud eclipsing
the half moons of my nails,
eclipse each startled eye, each
dedicated sleep.

Library of Congress Cataloging in Publication Data

Stewart, Susan.
  Yellow stars and ice.

  (Princeton series of contemporary poets)
  I. Title.
PS3569.T474Y4   811'.54   80-8587
ISBN 0-691-06468-7
ISBN 0-691-01379-9 (pbk.)